If I Were a Kid in Ancient Greece

Cricket Books
Peterborough, NH

Staff

Editorial Director: Lou Waryncia

Editor: Ken Sheldon

Book Design: David Nelson, www.dnelsondesign.com

Designer: Ann Dillon

Proofreader: Eileen Terrill

Text Credits

The content of this volume is derived from articles that first appeared in *AppleSeeds, Calliope,* and *DIG* magazines. Contributing writers: Nancy Barton, John Camp, Stephen Currie, Ann Jordan, Kathiann M. Kowalski, R. Anthony Kugler, Carl Meister, Jenifer Neils, Mary Northrup, John H. Oakley, Jane Sutcliffe, Brian Walsh, Mike Weinstein.

Picture Credits

Photos.com: Cover; Photo-Objects.net: Cover; Shutterstock: Cover, 1, 3, 4, 5 (bottom); Greek National Tourist Office: 5 (top); The Metropolitan Museum of Art, Rogers Fund, 1907 (07.286.4) Photograph © 2002 Metropolitan Museum of Art: 8; The J. Paul Getty Museum: 10 (top); The J. Paul Getty Museum, Gift of Arthur Silver: 10 (middle); Malibu, California, The J. Paul Getty Museum, Gift of Nicolas Koutoulakis: 10 (bottom); Zurich, Leo Mildenberg Collection: 11 (top); Réunion des Musées Nationaux / Art Resource, NY: 11 (middle); Erich Lessing / Art Resource, NY: 11 (bottom), 12, 17, 22; North Wind Picture Archives: 12–13; The Metropolitan Museum of Art, Samuel P. Avery Memorial Fund, 1923 (23.259) Photograph © 2002 The Metropolitan Museum of Art: 13; The Metropolitan Museum of Art, The Cesnola Collection, purchased by subscription, 1874–76 (74.51.5495), all rights reserved: 14; Brunswick, Maine, Bowdoin College Museum of Art, Gift of Edward Perry Warren, Esq. Honorary Degree, 1926, 1913.01:15; University of California, Berkeley, Nemea Excavation Archives: 16, 20, 21; Nimatallah / Art Resource, NY: 18; Hood Museum of Art, Dartmouth College, Hanover, NH, gift of Mr. and Mrs. Ray Winfield Smith, Class of 1918: 19; Clipart.com: 26.

Illustration Credits

Lynn Jeffery: 6, 7 (top), 27; John Gordon-Swogger: 7 (bottom); Chris Wold Dyrud: 9; Cheryl Jacobsen: 23; Mark Mitchell: 24–25, 26; Kathryn Adams: 28–29.

Library of Congress Cataloging-in-Publication Data

If I were a kid in ancient Greece / Lou Waryncia, editorial director; Ken Sheldon, editor. — 1st ed.

   p. cm. — (Children of the ancient world)

   ISBN-13: 978-0-8126-7929-8 (hardcover)

   ISBN-10: 0-8126-7929-6 (hardcover)

   1. Children—Greece—Juvenile literature. 2. Greece—Civilization—To 146 B.C.—Juvenile literature. 3. Greece—Social life and customs—Juvenile literature. I. Waryncia, Lou. II. Sheldon, Kenneth M. III. Series.

   DF93.I35 2006

   938—dc22   2006014673

Cricket Books

a division of Carus Publishing

30 Grove Street, Suite C

Peterborough, NH 03458

www.cricketmag.com

Printed in China

Table of Contents

Gifts from the Greeks

The Parthenon looks down over modern Athens, just as it did during the height of ancient Greece, from the 5th to the 2nd century B.C.

What kind of gum do you like—grape, spearmint, or mastic? Kids in ancient Greece didn't have a choice. They collected sticky sap from the mastic tree and chewed it, just as we chew bubblegum today.

If you lived in the ancient city-state of Athens, you could look and see the white columns of the Parthenon. The Athenians built this temple on top of the Acropolis, the hill overlooking the city. They dedicated it to the goddess Athena. Architects all over the world have copied Greek designs.

Have you ever been to a theater where live plays are performed? In ancient Greece, there were huge open-air theaters that held more than 10,000 people.

Drama was a Greek invention. The word "drama" comes from the Greek word for "action." Greek writers wrote the first tragedies (sad plays) and comedies (funny plays). Some of those ancient plays are still performed today.

Power to the People

Our system of democracy also has its roots in ancient Greece. The Athenians believed it was important for all citizens to be involved in their government. However, only men 18 years old or older were allowed to be citizens. Today, the United States has a democracy, too. When you turn 18, you can vote in elections.

Have you watched the Olympic Games or seen a marathon race? The first Olympic Games were held more than 2,500 years ago in Olympia, in western Greece. The games were held every four years to honor the great god Zeus.

The first marathon was a communication event, not a sporting event. Messages in ancient Greece were carried by men who could run the long distances between cities. Phidippides, a famous Athenian messenger, ran about 26 miles from Marathon to Athens with an important message. Today's marathon races, which are also 26 miles long, were named for his amazing run. Maybe you'll train to run in a marathon race someday. When you do, remember the gifts of the Greeks.

A modern runner passes through the entrance to the ancient grounds of the Olympic Games.

Greek actors wore masks that showed emotions of joy, sorrow, or anger.

House Rules

Wipe your feet! Wear your helmet! Practice the piano! Does it feel like someone is always telling you what to do? Don't feel bad. In ancient Greece, parents ruled over their children with a firm hand. If you were a kid then, here are some of the rules you would have had to obey.

Recite your lessons!

Education was very important. Many boys even had their own private teachers. Their lessons included poetry, history, and philosophy. Girls were taught at home by their mothers.

Go practice your lyre!

Music was very important. Almost all kids played an instrument. Some kids practiced their lyres, double-pipes, or horns for three hours every day!

Go to the gym!

Boys went to the gym to become strong and fit. And they wrestled naked!

Go to the temple!

Greeks worshipped many gods. Families often went to the temples together to offer gifts, but sometimes kids went by themselves.

Be brave!

So you don't want to go to the temple by yourself or fight in the mock battle? Too bad. Boys and girls in ancient Greece were expected to be brave in all kinds of danger.

Home, Sweet Home

What was it like to live in an ancient Greek house? Most houses were built around a large open courtyard. The rooms were arranged to let in as much daylight as possible. City houses were small, with just two or three rooms. Country houses had as many as a dozen rooms. The houses were built of inexpensive materials, such as sun-dried mud bricks. The walls were plastered or painted—white, red, yellow, and black were the favorite colors. The Greeks also decorated their walls with fabric hangings or wall paintings. Most houses had packed-earth or stone floors, but a few were finished with mosaics, colored bits of glass or stone.

Bronze Fly & Sheep Bones

Just like kids today, the children of ancient Greece played with many kinds of toys. In excavations of Greek houses, archaeologists have found tops, marbles, wagons, and clay figurines of people and animals. As babies, Greek children were given rattles, often in the shape of animals. When they became a little older, they might ride on a rocking horse. Greek children made up ball games too, but their ball was made of wool. They played with hoops, swings, seesaws, and yo-yos. They also played games with dice and sheep's knucklebones (like our jacks).

The ancient Greeks had games similar to hide and seek or tag. In a game called bronze fly, one child was blindfolded and then tried to catch the others. In another game, two teams threw a broken piece of pottery up into the air. If its black side landed up, the Nights team chased the Days team. If the other side landed up, the Days did the chasing.

Greek kids also played board games. One of these was similar to checkers or chess. Players moved pieces made of metal or glass across a board divided into squares, trying to corner the other players' pieces so they couldn't move.

In 300 B.C., Greek children played a game called *ephidrismos*, which was like our piggyback (opposite).

There were pull toys made of wood, clay, or leather, in the shapes of riding figures, animals, and carts. Girls played with dolls that had movable arms and legs.

How do we know about games and toys from thousands of years ago? From the pictures on vases and

Bones as Toys

A long with more active sports, Greek boys and girls also played quieter games, many of which used dice called *astragaloi*, or "knucklebones." At first, these were actually made from the ankle bones of sheep or goats. Later, they were made of clay, metal, and other materials. Each of the bones had four sides, and each side had a value.

Knucklebones could be used to determine your move in a board game, or by themselves in betting games. In these games, a player generally threw four knucklebones at a time. The best possible outcome was the "throw of Venus," in which each of the four possible values appeared once. The worst was the "Chian throw," named after the island of Chios. In this case, all four bones came up with a value of one. Adults played knucklebones too, sometimes gambling away large sums of money. Others used them to predict the future. But nobody loved to play knucklebones more than kids.

A drawing from a Greek vase shows boys playing knucklebones. They could have used real bones or the metal or glass versions shown here.

stone carvings made in ancient Greece, and from the toys that archaeologists have found.

When children became teenagers, they took their toys to the temple and dedicated them to the goddess Artemis and the god Hermes. The children knew it was time to put away the games of children and become adults.

This top and horse-shaped pull toy aren't that different from toys children play with today.

Pet Pals

Greek children were devoted to their pets, which were common in the world of Greece. Dogs were their favorite. (Cats didn't become household pets until very late in the history of Greece.) Birds were another favorite, especially doves, pigeons, and geese. This Greek vase from 425 B.C. shows a boy playing with his dog.

School Days

What was it like to go to school in ancient Greece? What would you study? That depended on where you lived and whether you were a boy or a girl. In ancient Greece, there were no rules about how long students had to stay in school or what they studied.

In Athens, children were taught at home by their parents, nurses, and slaves until they were 6 or 7. Then everything changed. The girls stayed at home, where the older women taught them how to run a household. They learned to spin wool into yarn and weave it into cloth. They also learned to cook and sew. Mothers taught daughters the reading, writing, and math skills they would need to keep lists of household supplies.

Boys, on the other hand, went to school—if their parents could pay for it. There was no free public education in Athens. At school, boys learned to read, write, and do math problems. That may sound familiar,

Students in ancient Greece were escorted to school by a family slave known as the *paidagogos*.

A scene from a Greek drinking cup shows a student getting a lesson on the *aulos* (left) and another student writing on a tablet (middle).

but their school supply list was quite different from yours. Students wrote on wax tablets and did math problems with an abacus, rows of beads on a frame. In music class, they strummed a lyre—a kind of harp—while they recited poetry or sang. Sometimes they played a flutelike instrument called the *aulos*. And half of every day was spent practicing sports such as gymnastics, wrestling, and throwing the javelin and discus.

An elderly Greek teacher wonders if his student will ever understand the lesson.

School started early in the morning and lasted until the afternoon, when students returned home for lunch. A tutor or guardian went along with each student, usually an older slave known as the *paidagogos*. There were also special teachers for music (the *kitharistes*), physical education (the *paidotribes*) and reading, writing, and arithmetic (the *grammatistes*). The Greeks believed that training the mind and the body were equally important.

> Greek students learned their alphabet backward and forward.

When Greek students learned to read, they first memorized the Greek alphabet until they could recite it backward and forward. Next, they learned to write their names. From there, they moved on to copying exercises. First they made copies of lists, then short passages, and eventually long passages. More advanced students had writing and grammar exercises. Greek students also had to memorize and recite works by the great poets, including the *Iliad* and the *Odyssey* by the great poet Homer.

How do we know all this? Again, from looking at painted Greek vases, which show students practicing their writing, playing music, singing, reciting, and competing in sports. Archaeologists have also found writing on fragments of pottery, painted wooden boards, and pieces of papyrus (a kind of paper made from a grassy plant)—exercises that Greek students completed centuries ago!

A Greek student used the pointed end of this stylus to write on a wax tablet, and the flat end to erase the writing. On the opposite page, a dance teacher corrects a student's steps.

For most boys, primary school ended when they were 14. But if you came from a wealthy Athenian family, you could go on to secondary school and study until you were 18. At that age, all boys had to perform two years of military service for the state. After that, the well-to-do could continue their educations by studying with such famous teachers as the philosopher Socrates and the orator Isocrates.

If you weren't rich, you would work with your father, learning a trade or helping him in the fields. The law said that every boy had to learn a trade. Girls who were slaves, foreigners, or from the lower classes were sometimes trained to entertain men at the *symposium*, where they would dance or play music for them.

Were They Smarter in Sparta?

Things were a little different in Sparta, another major Greek city-state. Sparta's schools were public rather than private. At age 6, students entered the *agoge*, the public educational system. The purpose of the *agoge* was to make warriors, not scholars. In some ways, the discipline and training in the *agoge* were like those of a modern military school.

Another big difference was that Spartan girls also received an education. So although school was hard in Sparta, it was more equal than in other places in ancient Greece.

Gym Class

The New Nemean
Races are held every
four years at the site
of the ancient foot-
races. These days,
everyone can take
part, young and old.

I magine you're a boy living in Athens 2,500 years ago. Sure it's a democracy, but you have to go to school, while your sister gets to stay at home and learn to cook and sew. Still, it's good to get out of the *oiko*s ("home"), even if you have to be accompanied by your old tutor, the *paidagogos*. The best part about school is that it is not all reading, writing, or learning to play the lyre. There's also plenty of time devoted to gym class!

You may not believe that gym existed that long ago, but the English word "gym" is short for "gymnasium," which comes from the Greek word *gymnos*, meaning "naked." Boys would strip down to nothing to train under the watchful eye of a special coach (*paidotribes*) in the hope that they might someday compete in the great festival of Zeus held at Olympia.

Gym class in ancient Athens was serious business. Athenians believed that a healthy body was as important as a healthy mind, and gym class occupied a few hours each day.

The word "gym" comes from the Greek word for naked!

Games for Girls

Girls did not compete in the ancient Olympics. In fact, women were not even allowed to watch the games on pain of death! But there was a special footrace for girls. It was held in the Olympic stadium every four years in honor of Zeus' wife, the goddess Hera. The race course was shorter than the normal distance, and the winners were given a crown of olive leaves.

Many of the competitors were probably girls from the Greek city-state of Sparta. The Spartans encouraged their women to do the same exercises as men. They believed that stronger children came from parents who were both well-built.

Athens may have had athletics for girls, too. A series of special Athenian vases shows girls running around an altar of the goddess Artemis. Generally, however, girls spent most of their time indoors helping their mothers cook, weave, and tend the other children in the family.

Athenian boys didn't play many team sports such as soccer or basketball. Instead, they practiced individual contests, many of them like today's track events. Running contests were held on soft sand. When boys did the long jump, they held weights in each hand. They also competed in the javelin toss. The javelin looked like a spear without a sharp point. The farthest throw was the winner. The longest throw also won in the discus-hurling contest. The discus was like a heavy Frisbee.

Wrestling was probably the favorite sport because it used many muscles. Before the boys started practicing, they took off all their clothes and rubbed special oil onto their bodies. A dark suntan was a mark of distinction for boys and grown men.

Wrestling was one of the most popular sports for young men in ancient Greece. The wrestlers were covered with oil, which made it hard to get a grip on each other.

Together, the five events of running, discus, long jump, javelin, and wrestling made up the *pentathlon*. (*Penta* is Greek for "five.")

Gym class was held in a *palaestra*, an outdoor arena. The gym class didn't sound like one today, though. To boost the spirits of the gym class, at least one boy played music while the others practiced their sports.

A Greek Gym Bag

This ancient image (from the inside of a Greek wine cup) shows a boy named Epidromos surrounded by his gym equipment. Epidromos is getting ready to box, so he is wrapping his left hand and wrist with a long strip of leather. This would protect his hand during boxing, but not his head. Greek boxers did not wear helmets, so he was likely to suffer a bloody nose at the very least.

The big round circle is a discus for throwing. The two black objects at his feet are lead jumping weights, which helped propel athletes farther in the long jump. The pick on Epidromos' left was used to loosen the ground so he would have a soft landing.

Athletes would rub their bodies with olive oil to keep them supple. Next to Epidromos' elbow is a little, round oil flask with a bull's-eye on it. Behind the flask is a thin curving line that represents a *strigil*. The strigil was a kind of spatula used to scrape the dirty oil off the skin after exercising.

Let's Go to the Games!

The Olympics, which began in Greece in 776 B.C., are the most famous games in the world. But they weren't the only competitions in ancient Greece. There were three other big events, held at the sanctuaries of Poseidon at Isthmia, Zeus at Nemea, and Apollo at Delphi. At these "crown" events, there was only a first-place winner. Each winner received a wreath. At Olympia, the wreath was made of olive leaves, at Isthmia it was pine, at Nemea it was celery, and at Delphi it was laurel.

The original Olympics were held in Olympia, near the Temple of Zeus. This model shows what the temple looked like in 776 B.C.

There were running contests, the pentathlon, wrestling, boxing, and the *pankration*—wrestling with no rules except that biting and gouging were forbidden. Kicking, punching, strangling, and even breaking bones were all allowed. The winner was the contestant who didn't pass out or die. Another event was a race in armor—that's tough!

Each site had a stadium about 656 feet long—longer than two football fields—for the footraces and the pentathlon. Horse and chariot racing took place farther away in a *hippodrome*, a Greek word meaning "horse track." At Delphi, at the shrine of Apollo, there were also contests in lyre playing and singing. Apollo was the god of music.

Not everyone could enter the Olympic contests. All the athletes were required to be male and Greek citizens. Women couldn't compete or watch, possibly because the athletes wore no clothes.

Each Greek city held elimination races to select

A device called the *hysplex* made sure that all the runners started at the same time. It has been re-created for the New Nemean Games. Runners stand with their toes in the grooves of the starting line. When the stretched cords of the *hysplex* snap to the ground, they're off!

the athletes who would represent them at Olympia. After ten months of training, finalists were chosen to compete in the games.

Olympic winners didn't pay taxes and got free food and lodging for life.

A winner at the Olympic Games was a hero for life. But the winner of the pentathlon, the five-event contest, became the grand champion and a hero for all time. Runners carried the news of his victory to his home city so they could celebrate. They would put up a bronze or marble statue of the champion, and send a second one to Olympia if the town could afford it. A famous poet would write a victory ode to immortalize the champion's feats. As the city's most honored citizen, the Olympic champion didn't have to pay taxes and was given free food and lodging for life.

The original Olympic Games ended in A.D. 393, after nearly 12 centuries of games. They provided the inspiration and the model for today's Olympic Games. The modern Olympics have many new events, and both men and women athletes come from all over the world to compete.

The winner of a footrace in ancient Athens might receive a decorated vase with a scene like this one, just as you might receive a trophy today.

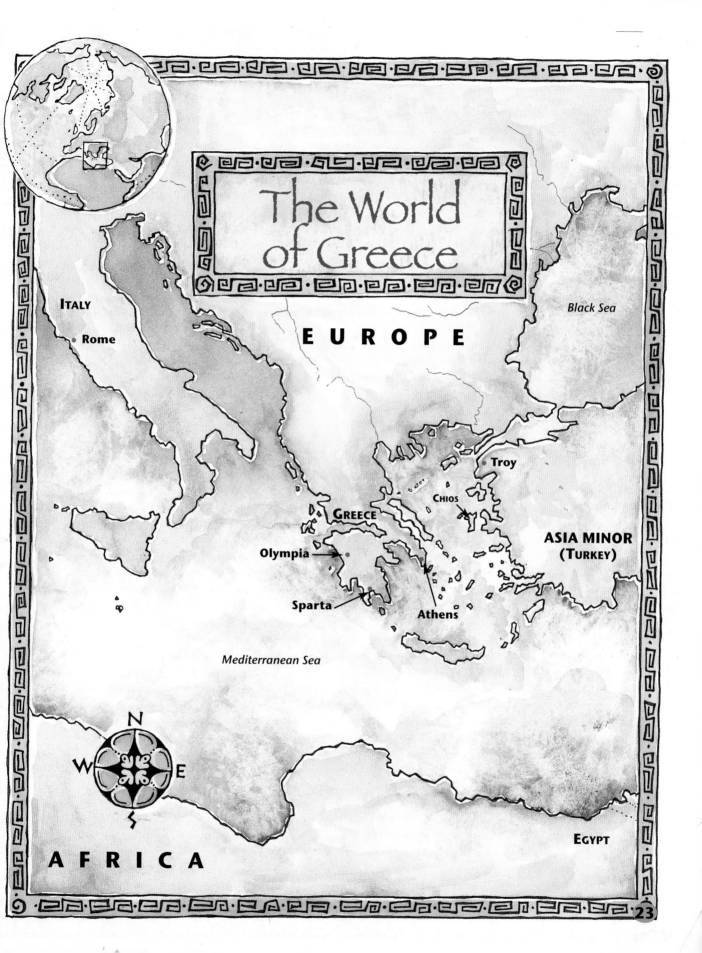

The World of Greece

ITALY

Rome

EUROPE

Black Sea

Troy

CHIOS

GREECE

ASIA MINOR
(TURKEY)

Olympia

Sparta

Athens

Mediterranean Sea

N

W E

S

EGYPT

AFRICA

An Ancient Hangout

Mmm! What is that delicious smell? It might be the aroma of freshly picked pomegranates, or perhaps the strong, sharp scent of well-aged goat cheese.

Follow your nose to the ancient *agora*, where you'll find all kinds of wonderful things to delight the senses.

The agora, or town center, is the heart of ancient Athens. It's where all the important matters of the city-state are discussed and voted upon. Young and old come to "hang out" with friends and hear the news of the day. Around the outskirts of the agora is the bustling marketplace. The agora is part village green, part supermarket, part country fair. Let's visit!

Just after dawn, it might seem that everyone else in town is headed to the agora, too. The narrow streets are a swirl of clothing dyed in colorful shades of red, yellow, green, and bright blue. In the marketplace itself, troupes of jugglers and acrobats keep the shoppers entertained.

What a confusion of noise! The calls of the vendors mix with the excited voices of people exchanging the latest gossip and arguing politics. But nearly all the voices you hear belong to men and boys. In ancient Greece, respectable women never go to the agora.

Farmers come to the marketplace with their goods to sell. You might try some sweet figs or ripe, salty olives. A sheep farmer has brought baskets of soft, fluffy fleece. The fishmonger's booth will make you wrinkle your nose. And there's no mistaking the smell of the goat vendor's stall.

The craftsmen of Athens show off their wares, too. The counter in the jeweler's shop sparkles with gold, silver, and bronze. The sandalmaker urges passersby to try on a new pair of sandals of the smoothest leather. At the toy seller's, you'll find clay rattles filled with pebbles to keep babies happy. There's something for everyone.

But people come to the agora for more than just shopping. One day they might be there to vote in an election, the next day it might be to watch athletic contests or a parade celebrating a religious festival. There is always something going on at the agora!

Pennies, Nickels... Drachmas!

If you wanted to buy something at the agora, you would have used coins. There was no paper money in ancient Greece. The two most important coins were the *drachma* and the *obol*. The value of money changed at different times, but usually one drachma equaled six obols.

Meet the Greek Gods

If you go to a church, synagogue, or mosque, you worship one God. But the ancient Greeks prayed to many gods. The Greek gods were a lot like humans—they fell in love, married, and had children. They had fun and they had fights. But they also had great power. Let's meet a few of the most important Greek gods.

Zeus—chief god, who ruled from Mount Olympus.

Hera—Zeus' jealous wife.

Athena—daughter of Zeus, she was the warrior goddess.

Apollo—god of the sun, music, poetry, archery, and medicine.

Artemis—Apollo's twin sister, she was the hunter goddess, and goddess of the moon.

Ares—god of war, son of Zeus and Hera.

Aphrodite—goddess of love and beauty.

Demeter—Zeus' sister, the goddess of farming.

Poseidon—Zeus' brother, who ruled the sea.

Hades—also Zeus' brother, ruler of the underworld, or land of the dead.

THIS WAY TO THE TEMPLE

Breakfast, Lunch, and Deipnon

How would you like to have dinner in an ancient Greek home? You might want to think before you answer.

Most Greeks ate very simple meals. *Akratisma,* or breakfast, was usually a piece of bread or a barley cake dipped in wine. In fact, bread was the biggest part of the Greek diet. It was usually made of wheat or barley.

Besides bread, the other main ingredients of a Greek meal were olive oil and wine, usually mixed with water. The Greeks used olive oil instead of butter, and honey instead of sugar as a sweetener.

Lunch (*ariston*) was simple, too, though maybe a bit heartier than breakfast. The Greeks were too busy to stop everything in the middle of the day just to eat. Along with the bread, they might have olives and fruits such as figs, apples, pears, or grapes.

The main meal of the day was the *deipnon,* served late in the day, often after sundown. Occasionally, the

Hist-O-Bit

The ancient Greeks looked down on people who ate too much or enjoyed their food too much.

Greeks would eat fish, birds, or wild game. If you were well-to-do, you could afford meat, but if you were poor you would eat meat only on special religious occasions. They would sacrifice a sheep, pig, or goat and distribute the meat to the people.

Spartan stew? No thank you!

If you were a Spartan, you would eat a stew called "black broth," made of pork, barley, salt, and vinegar. No wonder the Spartans were so tough!

The Greeks also ate a lot of fish, since they were surrounded by the sea, streams, and inlets. Along with herring, sardines, anchovies, and tuna, they also ate squid, eels, mussels, and turtles. The rich often dined on lobsters, scallops, crabs, and oysters.

You wouldn't find many vegetables at a Greek meal, although there were spinach, lettuce, lentils, and cabbage. There were also root vegetables such as radishes, onions, garlic, and leeks — but no potatoes, so no French fries!

The Greeks did not drink milk. They used it to make cheese. They weren't much for desserts, either. They ate walnuts, pine nuts, almonds, cakes made with honey, and cheesecakes.

If you were invited to a Greek meal, you would probably eat with your fingers. After eating, you would wipe your hands with pieces of bread and toss the "dirty" bread to the dogs. That made cleaning up easy!

Glossary

Abacus A device with beads strung on wires, used to do arithmetic.

Acropolis A fortified hill overlooking an ancient Greek city. In Athens, the Acropolis is the site of the Parthenon.

Agoge The public educational system of Sparta.

Agora A large open square where citizens gathered for shopping, meetings, and athletic events.

Akratisma Breakfast in ancient Greece.

Archaeologist A person who studies ancient times by exploring fossils, relics, and ruins.

Ariston The midday meal in ancient Greece.

Astragaloi Dice used to play games, also known as knucklebones.

Aulos A flutelike instrument.

City-state A powerful city and the territory it controlled. Athens and Sparta were city-states.

Deipnon The main, evening meal in ancient Greece.

Democracy Rule by the people, from the Greek words for "people" *(demos)* and "power" *(kratos)*.

Drachma An ancient Greek silver coin.

Grammatistes A reading, writing, and arithmetic teacher.

Hippodrome Greek arena for horse and chariot racing.

Hysplex Starting mechanism for ancient footraces.

Iliad and **Odyssey** Long, epic poems by the renowned poet Homer.

Kitharistes A music teacher.

Lyre A harplike stringed instrument used to accompany singing or poetry.

Marathon A 26-mile cross-country footrace.

Mosaics Decorations made by placing small, colored pieces of stone, glass, or ceramic to form a picture or a pattern.

Obol An ancient Greek silver coin equal to one-sixth of a drachma.

Olympia Site of the ancient Olympic Games and the Temple of Zeus, one of the Seven Wonders of the World.

Olympics Athletic event held every four years in Greece from 776 B.C. to A.D. 393. The modern Olympics began in 1896 in Athens.

Paidagogos A student's tutor or guardian, usually an older slave.

Paidotribes A physical education teacher.

Palaestra An outdoor arena for wrestling, races, and other athletic events.

Pankration A violent wrestling match with few rules, often ending in death.

Parthenon The temple of the goddess Athena in Athens.

Pentathlon An athletic event consisting of five events: running, discus toss, long jump, javelin toss, and wrestling.

Strigil A tool used to scrape the skin after exercising or bathing.

Tunic A loose garment worn by both men and women in ancient Greece.

Index

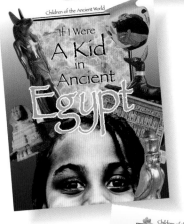